HOW BIG IS
AN ELEPHANT?

HOW BIG IS
AN ELEPHANT?

Text and illustrations by Rossana Bossù

annick press
toronto + berkeley

ONTARIO ARTS COUNCIL
CONSEIL DES ARTS DE L'ONTARIO
an Ontario government agency
un organisme du gouvernement de l'Ontario

Cataloguing in Publication

Bossù, Rossana, 1971-
[Quanto è grande un elefante? English]
     How big is an elephant? / Rossana Bossù.

Translation of: Quanto è grande un elefante?
Issued in print and electronic formats.
ISBN 978-1-55451-998-9 (hardcover).--ISBN 978-1-55451-997-2 (softcover).--
ISBN 978-1-55451-999-6 (PDF)

     1. Ratio and proportion--Juvenile literature. 2. Body size--Juvenile
literature. 3. Zoo animals--Juvenile literature. I. Title. II. Title: Quanto
è grande un elefante? English.

QA117.B6813 2018   j513.2›4   C2017-905617-4
                                              C2017-905618-2

Published in the U.S.A. by Annick Press (U.S.) Ltd.
Distributed in Canada by University of Toronto Press.
Distributed in the U.S.A. by Publishers Group West.

Printed in China

www.annickpress.com
www.rossanabossu.blogspot.it

Please visit www.annickpress.com/ebooks.html for more details.

To Giacomo

1

POLAR BEAR
IS SMALLER
THAN AN

YOU NEED
7 POLAR BEARS
TO MAKE AN ELEPHANT

1

LION
IS SMALLER
THAN A

YOU NEED 4 LIONS
TO MAKE
A POLAR BEAR

1

ALLIGATOR
IS SMALLER
THAN A

YOU NEED **3** ALLIGATORS
TO MAKE A LION

1

PENGUIN
IS SMALLER
THAN AN

YOU NEED 5 PENGUINS

TO MAKE AN ALLIGATOR

1

LEMUR
IS SMALLER
THAN A

YOU NEED

10 LEMURS

TO MAKE

A PENGUIN

1

FLEA

IS SMALLER

THAN A

AN ELEPHANT IS BIG

A FLEA IS SMALL

BUT WHAT
IS MUCH,
MUCH, MUCH
BIGGER
THAN BOTH?

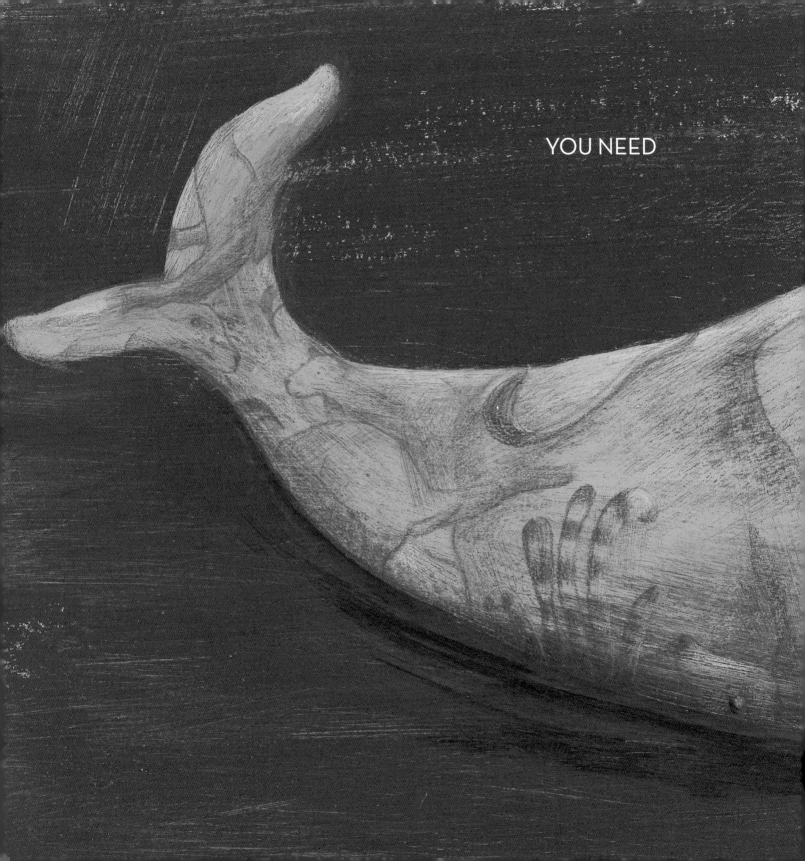

YOU NEED

7 ELEPHANTS, 6 POLAR BEARS, 2 LIONS, 4 ALLIGATORS,
9 PENGUINS, 10 LEMURS, AND 1 FLEA

TO MAKE A WHALE

ROSSANA BOSSÙ was born in Turin, Italy in 1971. She now lives with her husband and son in a small town surrounded by forests and mountains. Before she turned to illustrating children's books, she worked as a freelance graphic designer for advertising and editing agencies. What she loves most about creating picture books is the opportunity to express her love for nature, animals, and plants. Rossana has won a number of international awards for her work.